# 31 Habits of Champions:

## Your 31-Day Journey to Greatness

*Gerard Assey*

**31 Habits of Champions:**
**Your 31-Day Journey to Greatness**

By

Gerard Assey



*Published by:*
Gerard Assey
19/18, Palli Arasan Street
Anna Nagar East
Chennai - 600 102

**ISBN:** 978-93-92492-71-6



*(Image courtesy macrovector on Freepik: 'https://www.freepik.com' Thank You)*

# Table of Contents

# Preface

Welcome to **'31 Habits of Champions: Your 31-Day Journey to Greatness'**- an exploration of the habits that set champions apart and paves the way to success in various domains of life. In this book, we delve into the essential habits that champions embody, drawing inspiration from the stories of remarkable individuals who have achieved greatness.

Champions are not born overnight. They are made through a combination of unwavering commitment, discipline, and a relentless pursuit of excellence. Whether you aspire to become a champion in sports, business, arts, or any other field, this book offers valuable insights into the habits that can help you unlock your full potential.

The 31 Habits are divided into 6 essential parts that will help you in your journey towards being a Champion- with each day focusing on a specific habit, by exploring its importance, with real-life examples of successful individuals who have exemplified it, and offering practical steps to help you develop and integrate these habits into your own life. From goal setting and discipline to resilience, adaptability, and continuous improvement, each habit is dissected to provide a clear roadmap for personal growth and achievement. Implementing the 31 habits by practicing one habit a day over the course of a month can be an effective way to develop and integrate these habits into your life

It is essential to understand that the journey to champion status is not without its challenges. Champions face setbacks, failures, and obstacles along the way. However, it is their unwavering commitment to these key habits that propels them forward, allowing them to rise above adversity and reach new heights.

As you embark on your own journey of self-improvement and success, this small, yet power-packed book aims to be your guide, providing you with the knowledge, inspiration, and practical steps needed to develop and imbibe these crucial habits. By cultivating these habits in your own life, you can set yourself on a path towards personal fulfillment, excellence, and the realization of your goals.

Remember, becoming a champion is not solely about achieving external accolades or recognition. It is a deeply personal journey of self-discovery and growth. The habits outlined in this book are not just a means to an end but a way of life—a way to become the best version of yourself and leave a lasting impact on the world around you.

So, let us embark on this transformative journey together, exploring the 31 key habits of champions and may this book serve as a valuable resource, empowering you to embrace these habits, build on your potential, and claim your own place among the ranks of champions.

***Believe in yourself, commit to the process, and let the transformation begin today!***

## Why is it Important to Study and Emulate the Habits of Real-life Champions?

Studying and emulating the habits of real-life champions and successful individuals who have exhibited these habits in their own unique ways can be immensely valuable for personal growth and achievement. Here are several reasons why it is important to do so:

- ✓ Learning from Experience: Champions and successful individuals have achieved notable success in their respective fields through years of experience and hard work. By studying their habits, you gain access to a wealth of wisdom and insights accumulated over their journeys. For example, Warren Buffett's disciplined approach to investment, documented in his annual shareholder letters, provides valuable lessons for aspiring investors.
- ✓ Accelerating Growth: Emulating successful habits allows you to fast-track your own growth and development. By adopting proven strategies and behaviors, you can avoid common pitfalls and navigate challenges more effectively. For instance, entrepreneurs can learn from Elon Musk's ability to take calculated risks and embrace failure as a learning opportunity in order to drive innovation.
- ✓ Inspiring Motivation: Real-life champions serve as inspirations and role models. Their

achievements can motivate and inspire you to aim higher, dream bigger, and push past your limits. When faced with obstacles, knowing that others have overcome similar challenges can instill a sense of determination and resilience. For example, the story of Nelson Mandela's perseverance and forgiveness in the face of apartheid oppression continues to inspire people around the world.

- ✓ Developing a Winning Mindset: Champions possess a winning mindset that drives their actions and decisions. By studying their habits, you can develop a similar mindset, which includes qualities such as resilience, focus, and optimism. For instance, the unwavering determination of Serena Williams to overcome setbacks and consistently perform at a high level can inspire athletes to cultivate mental toughness.
- ✓ Enhancing Performance: The habits of champions are often directly linked to their exceptional performance. By studying and emulating these habits, you can enhance your own performance in various areas of life. For example, the meticulous preparation and attention to detail displayed by Kobe Bryant allowed him to excel on the basketball court, and athletes can adopt similar practices to improve their own performance.
- ✓ Cultivating Personal Excellence: Champions embody excellence in their actions, behaviors, and achievements. By emulating their habits, you cultivate a culture of excellence within yourself. Whether it's adopting Jeff Bezos' relentless pursuit of customer-centric

innovation or Beyoncé's dedication to honing her craft, emulating these habits pushes you to strive for greatness in your own pursuits.

- ✓ Leveraging Proven Strategies: Champions have developed effective strategies and approaches that have led to their success. By studying and emulating these strategies, you can benefit from their tested and proven methods. For example, Sheryl Sandberg's emphasis on leaning into challenges and fostering gender equality in the workplace provides valuable insights for aspiring leaders.
- ✓ Fostering Adaptability: Successful individuals often possess a remarkable ability to adapt to changing circumstances and embrace new opportunities. By observing and learning from their habits, you can cultivate adaptability in your own life. For instance, the way Angela Merkel navigated complex political situations and built strong international relationships can inspire individuals to develop diplomatic skills and adapt to dynamic environments.
- ✓ Developing Effective Leadership: Many champions and successful individuals exhibit exceptional leadership qualities. By studying their habits, you can glean insights into effective leadership behaviors such as communication, collaboration, and empathy. For example, the visionary leadership style of Bill Gates, combined with his ability to foster innovation, can provide guidance for aspiring leaders in the tech industry.
- ✓ Creating a Lasting Impact: Champions and successful individuals often leave a lasting impact on their industries and communities.

By studying their habits, you can understand the principles and values that underpin their impact. For example, Michelle Obama's dedication to empowering others, promoting education, and advocating for social change can inspire individuals to make a positive difference in the lives of others.

As can be seen, studying and emulating the habits of real-life champions and successful individuals allows you to leverage their experience, accelerate personal growth, cultivate a winning mindset, enhance performance, and create a lasting impact. By adopting their proven strategies and behaviors, you can navigate your own journey to success with greater clarity, purpose, and effectiveness.

# 31 Days Daily Action Plan to Making You a Champion!

Developing key habits is crucial for achieving success in any area of life. While there isn't a definitive list of habits that guarantee championship-level performance, here are 31 key habits that many champions embody.

Each habit is accompanied by its importance, examples, and steps to help you build and incorporate them into your life.

The 31 Habits are grouped into 6 parts as follows, to take you through a structured process:

*Part 1: Focus on Self-Development*
*Part 2: Cultivating Positive Behaviors*
*Part 3: Interpersonal Skills and Collaboration*
*Part 4: Personal Well-being and Success*
*Part 5: Growth and Reflection*
*Part 6: Feedback, Teamwork, and Reflection*

Implementing the 31 habits by practicing one habit a day over the course of a month can be an effective way to develop and integrate these habits into your life. So as you start on this exciting journey with the suggested schedule and steps of action to follow I am confident, that as you begin to implement it you will start to see yourself moving towards being and feeling like a Champion, with you being more productive and successful in every area of your life!

*Congratulations on this Journey towards becoming a Champion!*

# Part 1:
## Focus on Self-Development

# Day 1: Habit 1- Goal Setting

*"Champions keep playing until they get it right."* - **Billie Jean King**

Champions set clear, specific goals that provide direction and motivation. Example: Olympic athletes set specific performance goals to improve their skills.

**Example:** Serena Williams, a professional tennis player, has set clear and specific goals throughout her career, aiming to become the world's number one ranked player, win multiple Grand Slam titles, and achieve longevity in her sport.

**Steps:**

- ✓ Spend time reflecting on your short-term and long-term goals.
- ✓ Write them down and break them into actionable steps.
- ✓ Set specific targets for each goal.
- ✓ Your Goals must be SMARTER- Specific, Measurable, Achievable, Realistic/ Relevant, Time-bound, Exciting, Ready-Get, Set-Go!

**Summary:** Write down your long-term and short-term goals, break them into actionable steps, and track your progress regularly.

**Practical Exercises to Encourage Active Engagement and Facilitate Self-reflection**

Goal Setting Exercise: Create Your Vision Board Instructions:

- ✓ Gather magazines, newspapers, or print images from the internet that represent your short-term and long-term goals.

- ✓ Cut out these images and paste them on a large piece of paper or create a digital vision board using online tools.
- ✓ Write specific and measurable goals beside each image.
- ✓ Display your vision board in a prominent place where you can see it daily, reminding you of your aspirations.

**Your Turn:**

- ✓ *What Steps are you taking today in achieving this goal of becoming a Champion?*

# Day 2: Habit 2- Discipline

*"A champion is someone who gets up when they can't."* - **Jack Dempsey**

Champions maintain a strong work ethic and self-control to stay focused on their objectives. Example: Professional athletes follow strict training routines and dietary guidelines.

**Example:** Elon Musk, the CEO of Tesla and SpaceX, is known for his relentless work ethic and self-discipline. He maintains a rigorous schedule, adheres to strict timelines, and stays focused on his ambitious goals.

**Steps:**

- ✓ Identify areas in your life where you need more discipline.
- ✓ Set clear rules and routines to follow.
- ✓ Stay committed to these rules throughout the day.

**Summary:** Identify distractions, create a schedule, set deadlines, and practice self-restraint to develop discipline.

**Practical Exercises to Encourage Active Engagement and Facilitate Self-reflection**

Discipline Exercise: Establish Your Daily Routine Instructions:

- ✓ Identify the most critical activities that contribute to your goals.
- ✓ Design a daily schedule that allocates specific time blocks for these essential tasks.

- ✓ Set reminders or use time management apps to stay on track and follow your routine diligently.
- ✓ Evaluate your adherence to the routine weekly and make adjustments as needed for better discipline.

**Your Turn:**

*What Steps are you taking today in achieving this goal of becoming a Champion?*

# Day 3: Habit 3- Mental Toughness

*"Champions aren't made in the gyms. Champions are made from something they have deep inside them - a desire, a dream, a vision." -* ***Muhammad Ali***

Champions cultivate resilience to overcome challenges and setbacks. Example: Successful entrepreneurs persist through failures and learn from them.

**Example:** Michael Jordan, a basketball legend, demonstrated extraordinary mental toughness throughout his career. His resilience, determination, and ability to perform under pressure made him one of the greatest players in the history of the sport.

**Steps:**

- ✓ Recognize and acknowledge areas where you need to strengthen your mental resilience.
- ✓ Practice positive self-talk and develop strategies to overcome challenges.
- ✓ Focus on maintaining a positive and determined mindset.

**Summary:** Embrace failure as a learning opportunity, develop positive self-talk and affirmations, practice stress management techniques, and engage in regular mental and physical exercises.

**Practical Exercises to Encourage Active Engagement and Facilitate Self-reflection**

Mental Toughness Exercise: Journaling Resilience Instructions:

- ✓ Create a resilience journal to record challenging situations you encounter.
- ✓ Describe how you handled each situation and reflect on your emotions, thoughts, and actions.
- ✓ Identify patterns or areas for improvement in your responses.
- ✓ Develop strategies for cultivating mental toughness and write them down for future reference.

**Your Turn:**

*What Steps are you taking today in achieving this goal of becoming a Champion?*

# Day 4: Habit 4- Continuous Learning

*"Success is not the key to happiness. Happiness is the key to success. If you love what you are doing, you will be successful."* - **Albert Schweitzer**

Champions have a thirst for knowledge and actively seek opportunities to grow. Example: Renowned scientists constantly explore new research to expand their understanding.

**Example:** Warren Buffett, one of the most successful investors of all time, is renowned for his commitment to continuous learning. He continually reads, studies, and expands his knowledge to make informed investment decisions.

**Steps:**

- ✓ Identify a subject or skill you want to learn more about.
- ✓ Allocate time for reading, watching educational videos, or taking online courses.
- ✓ Engage in active learning and reflect on what you've learned.

**Summary:** Read books, attend seminars, listen to podcasts, take courses, and engage in discussions to broaden your knowledge base.

**Practical Exercises to Encourage Active Engagement and Facilitate Self-reflection**

Continuous Learning Exercise: Learning Bucket List

Instructions:

- ✓ List three to five subjects or skills you want to learn more about.

- ✓ Research educational resources such as books, online courses, or workshops related to each topic.
- ✓ Create a timeline for when you will begin each learning endeavor.
- ✓ As you complete each item on your learning bucket list, evaluate your progress and set new goals.

**Your Turn:**

*What Steps are you taking today in achieving this goal of becoming a Champion?*

## Day 5: Habit 5- Focus

*"Champions are not defined by their wins, but by how they recover when they fall."* - **Serena Williams**

Champions concentrate their energy and attention on the task at hand, minimizing distractions. Example: Chess grandmasters analyze the board and anticipate future moves without getting distracted.

**Example:** Novak Djokovic, a professional tennis player, showcases exceptional focus on the court. He maintains concentration, composure, and a laser-like focus during high-pressure situations, allowing him to consistently perform at a high level.

**Steps:**

- ✓ Choose a task or activity that requires your undivided attention.
- ✓ Minimize distractions and practice deep work.
- ✓ Concentrate fully on the task at hand and build your ability to stay focused.

**Summary:** Eliminate unnecessary distractions, practice mindfulness, set specific time blocks for deep work, and prioritize tasks.

**Practical Exercises to Encourage Active Engagement and Facilitate Self-reflection**

Focus Exercise: The 5-Minute Meditation Challenge

Instructions:

- ✓ Set aside five minutes each day for a simple meditation practice.
- ✓ Find a quiet and comfortable space to sit or lie down.

- ✓ Focus on your breath or a specific word or phrase (e.g., "calm" or "peace").
- ✓ Observe any thoughts that arise without judgment and gently bring your focus back to your breath or word.

**Your Turn:**
*What Steps are you taking today in achieving this goal of becoming a Champion?*

# Part 2:
## Cultivating Positive Behaviors

# Day 6: Habit 6- Perseverance

*"The difference between a successful person and others is not a lack of strength, not a lack of knowledge, but rather a lack in will."* - **Vince Lombardi**

Champions exhibit determination and tenacity to keep going despite difficulties. Example: Marathon runners push through physical exhaustion to reach the finish line.

**Example:** Oprah Winfrey, media mogul and philanthropist, overcame numerous obstacles and adversities on her path to success. Her perseverance, resilience, and unwavering determination played a significant role in her rise to prominence.

**Steps:**

- ✓ Select a challenging goal or task that requires persistence.
- ✓ Break it down into manageable steps and work on it consistently.
- ✓ Maintain a determined attitude even in the face of setbacks.

**Summary:** Develop a growth mindset, visualize success, break big goals into smaller milestones, and seek support from mentors or coaches.

**Practical Exercises to Encourage Active Engagement and Facilitate Self-reflection**

Perseverance Exercise: The Resilience Journal - Part 2 Instructions:

- ✓ Review your previous resilience journal entries.
- ✓ Identify the most challenging situations you've faced and your responses.
- ✓ Reflect on how you could have persevered even more effectively in those situations.
- ✓ Write a letter to your future self, encouraging perseverance in times of difficulty.

**Your Turn:**
*What Steps are you taking today in achieving this goal of becoming a Champion?*

# Day 7: Habit 7- Self-Reflection

*"A champion is someone who does not settle for that day's practice, that day's competition, that day's performance. They are always striving to be better." -* **Briana Scurry**

Champions regularly assess their performance to identify areas for improvement. Example: Musicians record their practice sessions and analyze their technique for refinement.

**Example:** Bill Gates, the co-founder of Microsoft, engages in regular self-reflection to assess his work and contributions. He actively seeks feedback, learns from his mistakes, and adjusts his strategies and approach accordingly.

**Steps:**

- ✓ Set aside time for introspection and self-assessment.
- ✓ Reflect on your actions, decisions, and progress.
- ✓ Identify areas for improvement and make necessary adjustments.

**Summary:** Journal your experiences, evaluate your strengths and weaknesses, seek feedback, and set aside time for self-assessment.

**Practical Exercises to Encourage Active Engagement and Facilitate Self-reflection**

Self-Reflection Exercise: Weekly Progress Tracker Instructions:

- ✓ Create a weekly progress tracker or use a spreadsheet to monitor your habits and goals.

- ✓ Set specific metrics to measure your progress in each area.
- ✓ Review your weekly performance and celebrate successes or identify areas for improvement.
- ✓ Adjust your approach for the upcoming week based on your reflections.

**Your Turn:**
*What Steps are you taking today in achieving this goal of becoming a Champion?*

# Day 8: Habit 8 - Resilience

*"Champions do not become champions when they win the event, but in the hours, weeks, months and years they spend preparing for it."* - **T. Alan Armstrong**

Champions bounce back from failures, setbacks, and adversity with strength and determination. Example: Resilient leaders navigate through difficult times and inspire their teams.

**Example:** Malala Yousafzai, a Nobel Peace Prize laureate, demonstrated remarkable resilience in the face of adversity. Despite surviving an assassination attempt by the Taliban, she continued her advocacy for girls' education, inspiring millions around the world.

**Steps:**

- ✓ Choose a situation or obstacle that typically causes stress or frustration.
- ✓ Practice resilience by reframing challenges as opportunities for growth.
- ✓ Stay calm, adaptable, and focused on finding solutions.

**Summary:** Build a support network, practice self-care, embrace challenges as learning opportunities, and develop a positive mindset.

**Practical Exercises to Encourage Active Engagement and Facilitate Self-reflection**

Resilience Exercise: Building Emotional Resilience Instructions:

- ✓ Identify emotions that tend to challenge your resilience, such as frustration or anxiety.

- ✓ Develop a toolbox of coping strategies, such as deep breathing, positive affirmations, or seeking support from loved ones.
- ✓ Practice using these coping mechanisms in situations that trigger difficult emotions.
- ✓ Keep a journal to track your emotional responses and your application of coping strategies.

**Your Turn:**
*What Steps are you taking today in achieving this goal of becoming a Champion?*

# Day 9: Habit 9 - Time Management:

*"Success is no accident. It is hard work, perseverance, learning, studying, sacrifice and most of all, love of what you are doing or learning to do." -* **Pelé**

Champions prioritize their tasks, maximize productivity, and make the most of their time. Example: CEOs efficiently allocate their time between strategic planning and execution.

**Example:** Indra Nooyi, the former CEO of PepsiCo, is known for her exceptional time management skills. She successfully balanced her professional responsibilities while prioritizing family life and personal interests.

**Steps:**

- ✓ Analyze your daily schedule and identify areas of inefficiency.
- ✓ Prioritize tasks and allocate time blocks for specific activities.
- ✓ Use time management techniques, such as the Pomodoro Technique, to enhance productivity.

**Summary:** Set clear priorities, create a schedule, break tasks into smaller chunks, eliminate time-wasting activities, and use productivity tools.

**Practical Exercises to Encourage Active Engagement and Facilitate Self-reflection**

Time Management Exercise: The 168-Hour Challenge Instructions:

- ✓ Map out how you spend your time over a typical week, accounting for all 168 hours.
- ✓ Analyze how much time you dedicate to essential tasks, hobbies, relaxation, etc.
- ✓ Identify areas where you can optimize your time allocation to align better with your goals.
- ✓ Create a revised weekly schedule that maximizes productivity and purposeful activities.

**Your Turn:**
*What Steps are you taking today in achieving this goal of becoming a Champion?*

## Day 10: Habit 10- Consistency

*"Champions believe in themselves even when no one else does."* - **Unknown**

Champions demonstrate a high level of consistency in their performance over time. Example: Professional golfers work on maintaining a consistent swing and accuracy.

**Example:** Tom Brady, an accomplished American football quarterback, has consistently performed at a high level throughout his career. His commitment to training, preparation, and self-discipline has led to numerous championships and individual accolades.

**Steps:**

- ✓ Select a habit or behavior you want to establish.
- ✓ Commit to performing it consistently throughout the day.
- ✓ Track your progress and hold yourself accountable.

**Summary:** Set achievable daily or weekly targets, establish routines, track progress, and review your performance regularly.

**Practical Exercises to Encourage Active Engagement and Facilitate Self-reflection**

Consistency Exercise: The 30-Day Consistency Challenge Instructions:

- ✓ Choose a habit you want to establish or strengthen.
- ✓ Commit to practicing this habit consistently for 30 days.

- ✓ Track your daily progress on a calendar or journal.
- ✓ Reflect on the impact of consistency on your overall performance and well-being.

**Your Turn:**

*What Steps are you taking today in achieving this goal of becoming a Champion?*

# Part 3:
## Interpersonal Skills and Collaboration

# Day 11: Habit 11- Adaptability

*"You are never really playing an opponent. You are playing yourself, your own highest standards, and when you reach your limits, that is real joy."* - **Arthur Ashe**

Champions adjust their strategies and approaches to changing circumstances. Example: Military leaders adapt their tactics based on the evolving battlefield conditions.

**Example:** Jeff Bezos, the founder of Amazon, is recognized for his adaptability and willingness to embrace new opportunities. He evolved Amazon from an online bookstore into a global e-commerce giant, constantly adapting to changing market dynamics.

**Steps:**

- ✓ Seek out a new experience or change your routine.
- ✓ Embrace the unfamiliar and practice adapting to different situations.
- ✓ Focus on being flexible and open-minded.

**Summary:** Embrace change, be open to new ideas, practice flexibility, seek diverse perspectives, and learn from different experiences.

**Practical Exercises to Encourage Active Engagement and Facilitate Self-reflection**

Adaptability Exercise: The Change-Ready Mindset

Instructions:

- ✓ Write down three recent changes or unexpected events you encountered.

- ✓ Reflect on your initial reactions and feelings toward these changes.
- ✓ Identify one positive aspect or opportunity that emerged from each situation.
- ✓ Practice reframing challenges as opportunities for growth and maintain an open and adaptable mindset.

**Your Turn:**
*What Steps are you taking today in achieving this goal of becoming a Champion?*

# Day 12: Habit 12 - Focus on Strengths

*"Champions are not afraid of losing. They are afraid of not giving it their all."* - **Unknown**

Champions identify and leverage their strengths to maximize their performance. Example: Successful entrepreneurs build businesses around their core competencies.

**Example:** Beyoncé, a multi-talented musician and performer, has built her career by leveraging her strengths in singing, dancing, and songwriting. She consistently showcases her unique talents, setting herself apart in the entertainment industry.

**Steps:**

- ✓ Identify your strengths and talents.
- ✓ Find ways to apply them in your daily activities or work projects.
- ✓ Delegate tasks that align with others' strengths, fostering teamwork.

**Summary:** Identify your strengths, delegate tasks that fall outside your expertise, seek opportunities to further develop your strengths, and align your goals accordingly.

**Practical Exercises to Encourage Active Engagement and Facilitate Self-reflection**

Focus on Strengths Exercise: The Strengths Discovery Instructions:

- ✓ Take a strengths assessment to identify your top strengths.

- ✓ Reflect on how you have applied these strengths in your personal and professional life.
- ✓ Set goals to leverage your strengths more intentionally in various aspects of your life.
- ✓ Share your strengths journey with a close friend or mentor for additional insights.

**Your Turn:**

*What Steps are you taking today in achieving this goal of becoming a Champion?*

# Day 13: Habit 13- Goal Visualization

*"The greatest glory in living lies not in never falling, but in rising every time we fall."* - **Nelson Mandela**

Champions vividly imagine themselves achieving their goals, enhancing motivation and confidence. Example: Visualizing a flawless gymnastics routine before the actual performance.

**Example:** Michael Phelps, the most decorated Olympian of all time, utilized goal visualization throughout his swimming career. He vividly imagined himself winning races and breaking records, harnessing the power of visualization to fuel his motivation and focus.

**Steps:**

- ✓ Visualize the successful completion of a specific goal or task.
- ✓ Use mental imagery to imagine yourself achieving it.
- ✓ Visualize the necessary steps and the positive emotions associated with accomplishment.

**Summary:** Create a mental image of your desired outcome, visualize the process and the emotions associated with success, and regularly reinforce these visualizations.

**Practical Exercises to Encourage Active Engagement and Facilitate Self-reflection**

Goal Visualization Exercise: The Visualization Practice Instructions:

- ✓ Set aside 5-10 minutes each day for visualization.

- ✓ Close your eyes and vividly imagine yourself achieving one of your most significant goals.
- ✓ Engage all your senses and immerse yourself in the experience of success.
- ✓ Journal your emotions and insights after each visualization session.

**Your Turn:**

*What Steps are you taking today in achieving this goal of becoming a Champion?*

# Day 14: Habit 14- Effective Communication

*"Champions are made from something they have deep inside them: a desire, a dream, a vision." -* **Mahatma Gandhi**

Champions convey their ideas, needs, and expectations clearly to achieve collaboration and alignment. Example: Inspirational speakers engage and motivate their audiences through effective communication.

**Example:** Sheryl Sandberg, the past COO of Facebook, is known for her effective communication skills. She articulates her ideas clearly, inspires teams, and advocates for gender equality in the workplace.

**Steps:**

- ✓ Choose a conversation or interaction where effective communication is crucial.
- ✓ Practice active listening, clear articulation, and empathy.
- ✓ Seek to understand others and express your thoughts effectively.

**Summary:** Develop active listening skills, practice clear and concise verbal and written communication, seek feedback, and adapt your communication style to different situations.

**Practical Exercises to Encourage Active Engagement and Facilitate Self-reflection**

Effective Communication Exercise: Active Listening Practice Instructions:

- ✓ Engage in a conversation with a friend, family member, or colleague.
- ✓ Practice active listening by giving your full attention and avoiding distractions.
- ✓ Ask clarifying questions to ensure a deeper understanding of their thoughts and feelings.
- ✓ Reflect on how active listening improves the quality of your interactions.

**Your Turn:**

*What Steps are you taking today in achieving this goal of becoming a Champion?*

# Day 15: Habit 15- Respecting and Valuing Others

*"Success is not final, failure is not fatal: It is the courage to continue that counts."* - **Winston Churchill**

Champions treat others with respect, fostering positive relationships and teamwork. Example: Successful team captains create a supportive and inclusive environment for their teammates.

**Example:** Nelson Mandela, a revered leader and activist, consistently demonstrated respect and value for others. He promoted inclusivity, forgiveness, and reconciliation during South Africa's transition from apartheid to democracy.

**Steps:**

- ✓ Engage in acts of kindness and appreciation towards others.
- ✓ Recognize and acknowledge their contributions or achievements.
- ✓ Foster an environment of respect and support.

**Summary:** Practice empathy, appreciate diverse perspectives, show gratitude, actively listen, and recognize the contributions of others.

**Practical Exercises to Encourage Active Engagement and Facilitate Self-reflection**

Respecting and Valuing Others Exercise: The Gratitude Challenge Instructions:

- ✓ Make a daily gratitude list, jotting down three things you are grateful for each day.

- ✓ Include moments when someone else's actions or presence made a positive impact on your day.
- ✓ Express your gratitude to those individuals and let them know how much you value them.
- ✓ Observe how showing appreciation strengthens your relationships.

**Your Turn:**

*What Steps are you taking today in achieving this goal of becoming a Champion?*

# Part 4:

## Personal Well-being and Success

# Day 16: Habit 16- Attention to Detail

*"Champions are not born, they are made. They are made by hard effort, which is the price which all of us must pay to achieve any goal that is worthwhile."* - **Vince Lombardi**

Champions pay close attention to every aspect of their craft, ensuring excellence. Example: Architects meticulously review blueprints to ensure accuracy and structural integrity.

**Example:** Tim Cook, the CEO of Apple, is known for his meticulous attention to detail in product design and user experience. He ensures that Apple's products maintain a high level of precision, aesthetics, and functionality.

**Steps:**

- ✓ Pick a task that requires careful attention and precision.
- ✓ Focus on executing it with meticulousness and accuracy.
- ✓ Double-check your work to ensure quality and thoroughness.

**Summary:** Develop a keen eye for detail, double-check your work, create checklists, and cultivate a mindset of thoroughness.

**Practical Exercises to Encourage Active Engagement and Facilitate Self-reflection**

Attention to Detail Exercise: The Observational Challenge Instructions:

- ✓ Choose an everyday object or scene and observe it closely for a few minutes.

- ✓ Take note of its details, colors, textures, and patterns.
- ✓ Sketch or describe what you observed, paying attention to even the smallest aspects.
- ✓ Practice this exercise regularly to sharpen your attention to detail.

**Your Turn:**

*What Steps are you taking today in achieving this goal of becoming a Champion?*

# Day 17: Habit 17- Health and Fitness

*"Success is not about winning everything, but making the effort to be the best that you can be."* - **Unknown**

Champions prioritize their physical well-being, recognizing its impact on overall performance. Example: Professional athletes maintain a balanced diet and regular exercise routine.

**Example:** Serena Williams, mentioned earlier, emphasizes the importance of health and fitness. She maintains a rigorous training regimen and prioritizes her physical well-being to sustain her peak performance on the tennis court.

**Steps:**

- ✓ Dedicate time to physical exercise or engage in a healthy activity.
- ✓ Prioritize nutritious meals and ensure sufficient rest and sleep.
- ✓ Take steps to maintain your overall well-being.

**Summary:** Engage in regular physical activity, adopt a healthy eating plan, get enough sleep, and prioritize self-care activities.

**Practical Exercises to Encourage Active Engagement and Facilitate Self-reflection**

Health and Fitness Exercise: The Wellness Commitment Instructions:

- ✓ Assess your current physical health and identify areas for improvement.
- ✓ Set specific fitness and nutrition goals that align with your overall well-being.

- ✓ Create an exercise and meal plan to support these goals.
- ✓ Track your progress and celebrate milestones in your health journey.

**Your Turn:**

*What Steps are you taking today in achieving this goal of becoming a Champion?*

## Day 18: Habit 18- Risk-Taking

*"Champions are willing to do what others won't." -* **Unknown**

Champions embrace calculated risks to seize opportunities and push beyond their comfort zones. Example: Innovators and entrepreneurs take calculated risks to bring disruptive ideas to market.

**Example:** Elon Musk, mentioned earlier, is recognized for his willingness to take calculated risks. His ventures, such as Tesla and SpaceX, involve significant technological and financial risks that have paid off with groundbreaking innovations.

**Steps:**

- ✓ Identify a calculated risk you have been hesitant to take.
- ✓ Weigh the potential rewards and consequences.
- ✓ Embrace the opportunity and take the necessary steps towards it.

**Summary:** Assess potential risks and rewards, gather information, consult with mentors or experts, and take calculated and informed risks.

**Practical Exercises to Encourage Active Engagement and Facilitate Self-reflection**

Risk-Taking Exercise: The Bold Move Instructions:

- ✓ Identify one calculated risk you've been hesitant to take.
- ✓ Weigh the potential rewards and consequences of this risk.

- ✓ Develop a plan to mitigate potential downsides and maximize positive outcomes.
- ✓ Take the bold move, embracing the opportunity and pushing beyond your comfort zone.

**Your Turn:**

*What Steps are you taking today in achieving this goal of becoming a Champion?*

# Day 19: Habit 19- Positive Attitude

*"Success is stumbling from failure to failure with no loss of enthusiasm."* - **Winston Churchill**

Champions maintain an optimistic outlook, even in the face of challenges. Example: Motivational speakers inspire others by radiating positivity and hope.

**Example:** Michelle Obama, the former First Lady of the United States, exudes a positive attitude and inspires optimism. Her messages of hope, empowerment, and inclusivity have resonated with people worldwide.

**Steps:**

- ✓ Practice positivity throughout the day.
- ✓ Notice negative thoughts and consciously reframe them.
- ✓ Cultivate gratitude and focus on the good in every situation.

**Summary:** Practice gratitude, challenge negative thoughts, surround yourself with positive influences, and cultivate an optimistic mindset.

**Practical Exercises to Encourage Active Engagement and Facilitate Self-reflection**

Positive Attitude Exercise: The Gratitude Journal Instructions:

- ✓ Keep a daily gratitude journal to write down three things you are thankful for each day.
- ✓ Focus on positive aspects even in challenging situations.

- ✓ Observe how expressing gratitude impacts your overall attitude and outlook on life.

**Your Turn:**
*What Steps are you taking today in achieving this goal of becoming a Champion?*

# Day 20: Habit 20- Humility

*"Champions keep playing until they get it right." -* **Billie Jean King**

Champions remain grounded and acknowledge the contributions of others to their success. Example: Accomplished musicians express gratitude to their mentors and acknowledge the work of their band mates.

**Example:** Satya Nadella, the CEO of Microsoft, demonstrates humility in his leadership style. He values diverse perspectives, fosters a collaborative work environment, and attributes success to the collective efforts of his team.

**Steps:**

- ✓ Engage in acts of humility and genuine humility towards others.
- ✓ Acknowledge others' contributions and admit mistakes.
- ✓ Seek feedback and be open to learning from others.

**Summary:** Embrace a growth mindset, seek feedback, recognize the accomplishments of others, and maintain humility in both success and failure.

**Practical Exercises to Encourage Active Engagement and Facilitate Self-reflection**

Humility Exercise: The Humility Challenge Instructions:

- ✓ Practice acts of humility in your daily interactions.

- ✓ Listen more than you speak and show genuine interest in others' perspectives.
- ✓ Accept feedback graciously and acknowledge your mistakes.
- ✓ Reflect on how practicing humility enhances your relationships and leadership abilities.

**Your Turn:**
*What Steps are you taking today in achieving this goal of becoming a Champion?*

# Part 5:
## Growth and Reflection

# Day 21: Habit 21- Networking

*"It's not whether you get knocked down; it's whether you get up."* - **Vince Lombardi**

Champions build strong professional relationships, creating opportunities for collaboration and growth. Example: Successful entrepreneurs expand their networks to gain support and access resources.

**Example:** Richard Branson, the founder of Virgin Group, is known for his exceptional networking skills. He has built extensive professional relationships and leveraged his network to drive strategic partnerships and business growth.

**Steps:**

- ✓ Reach out to a professional contact or join a networking event.
- ✓ Engage in meaningful conversations and establish connections.
- ✓ Foster mutually beneficial relationships.

**Summary:** Attend industry events, join professional organizations, build relationships through social media platforms, and initiate conversations with like-minded individuals.

**Practical Exercises to Encourage Active Engagement and Facilitate Self-reflection**

Networking Exercise: The Networking Event

Instructions:

- ✓ Attend a networking event, whether in-person or virtual.

- ✓ Engage in meaningful conversations with new people, actively listening to their interests and goals.
- ✓ Exchange contact information and follow up with those you connected with.
- ✓ Continue nurturing these connections and offering support when possible.

**Your Turn:**

*What Steps are you taking today in achieving this goal of becoming a Champion?*

# Day 22: Habit 22- Emotional Intelligence

*"Champions are willing to push themselves when no one else is watching."* - **Unknown**

Champions understand and manage their emotions and effectively navigate social interactions. Example: Effective leaders inspire and motivate their teams by demonstrating empathy and emotional awareness.

**Example:** Angela Merkel, the former Chancellor of Germany, exhibited emotional intelligence in her leadership. She effectively managed complex political situations, demonstrated empathy, and built strong international relationships.

**Steps:**

- ✓ Practice emotional intelligence in a challenging situation.
- ✓ Regulate your emotions, empathize with others, and communicate effectively.
- ✓ Seek a win-win outcome in conflicts.

**Summary:** Practice self-awareness, develop empathy, regulate emotions, improve active listening skills, and seek feedback on your emotional impact on others.

**Practical Exercises to Encourage Active Engagement and Facilitate Self-reflection**

Emotional Intelligence Exercise: The Emotional Awareness Journal Instructions:

- ✓ Keep a journal to track your emotions throughout the day.

- ✓ Identify patterns in your emotional responses and the triggers behind them.
- ✓ Practice emotional regulation techniques, such as deep breathing or taking short breaks.
- ✓ Evaluate how improved emotional intelligence positively impacts your relationships.

**Your Turn:**

*What Steps are you taking today in achieving this goal of becoming a Champion?*

# Day 23: Habit 23 - Preparation

*"Success is not measured by what you accomplish, but by the opposition you have encountered, and the courage with which you have maintained the struggle against overwhelming odds."* - **Orison Swett Marden**

Champions invest time and effort in thorough preparation, enabling peak performance. Example: Public speakers rehearse their speeches and anticipate potential questions.

**Example:** Kobe Bryant, mentioned earlier, was known for his meticulous preparation. He would study opponents' game-play, analyze their weaknesses, and devise strategies to exploit them. Bryant's thorough preparation gave him a competitive edge on the basketball court.

Steps:

- ✓ Choose an upcoming task or event and invest time in thorough preparation.
- ✓ Research, plan, and equip yourself with the necessary knowledge and resources.
- ✓ Increase your confidence and readiness for success.

**Summary:** Research and gather information, practice skills, create checklists, simulate scenarios, and prepare mentally and physically for upcoming challenges.

**Practical Exercises to Encourage Active Engagement and Facilitate Self-reflection**

Preparation Exercise: The Preparedness Checklist

Instructions:

- ✓ Create a checklist for preparing for significant events or projects.
- ✓ Research, plan, and gather resources well in advance to ensure smooth execution.
- ✓ Regularly update the checklist based on new experiences and insights.
- ✓ Observe how thorough preparation increases your confidence and success rate.

**Your Turn:**

*What Steps are you taking today in achieving this goal of becoming a Champion?*

# Day 24: Habit 24- Self-Care

*"Champions are not those who never fail, but those who never quit."* - **Unknown**

Champions prioritize their well-being, ensuring they have the physical and mental capacity to perform at their best. Example: Successful executives establish work-life balance and engage in activities that recharge them.

**Example:** Arianna Huffington, the co-founder of The Huffington Post, promotes the value of self-care. She emphasizes the importance of sleep, mindfulness, and work-life balance for overall well-being and success.

**Steps:**

- ✓ Prioritize self-care activities that promote your well-being.
- ✓ Engage in activities that relax and rejuvenate you.
- ✓ Ensure a healthy work-life balance and establish boundaries.

**Summary:** Identify activities that bring you joy and relaxation, establish boundaries, practice stress management techniques, and allocate time for self-care activities.

**Practical Exercises to Encourage Active Engagement and Facilitate Self-reflection**

Self-Care Exercise: The Self-Care Routine Instructions:

- ✓ Develop a self-care routine that includes activities promoting physical, emotional, and mental well-being.
- ✓ Schedule dedicated time for self-care on a daily or weekly basis.
- ✓ Prioritize your self-care needs without guilt or hesitation.
- ✓ Reflect on how consistent self-care enhances your overall performance and happiness.

**Your Turn:**
*What Steps are you taking today in achieving this goal of becoming a Champion?*

# Day 25: Habit 25- Accountability

*"The only way to do great work is to love what you do."* - **Steve Jobs**

Champions take responsibility for their actions, choices, and outcomes. Example: Team captains hold themselves accountable for their performance and take responsibility for the team's results.

**Example:** Tim Ferriss, entrepreneur, investor, author, podcaster, and lifestyle guru, demonstrates accountability by publicly sharing his progress and holding himself accountable to his audience. He inspires others to take action and achieve their goals.

**Steps:**

- ✓ Hold yourself accountable for a specific goal or commitment.
- ✓ Set measurable targets and track your progress.
- ✓ Take responsibility for your actions and make adjustments as needed.

**Summary:** Set clear expectations and goals, track your progress, accept feedback gracefully, learn from mistakes, and take ownership of your actions and their consequences.

**Practical Exercises to Encourage Active Engagement and Facilitate Self-reflection**

Accountability Exercise: The Accountability Partner

Instructions:

- ✓ Choose a trusted friend, colleague, or mentor to be your accountability partner.

- ✓ Share your goals and aspirations with them and seek their support.
- ✓ Schedule regular check-ins to discuss progress and challenges.
- ✓ Offer the same level of support and accountability to your partner.

**Your Turn:**

*What Steps are you taking today in achieving this goal of becoming a Champion?*

# Part 6:
## Feedback, Teamwork, and Reflection

# Day 26: Habit 26- Attention to Feedback

*"Champions are willing to work harder than anyone else."* - **Unknown**

Champions actively seek and value feedback as a means for growth and improvement. Example: Professional athletes work closely with coaches and trainers to refine their technique based on feedback.

**Example:** Mary Barra, the CEO of General Motors, actively seeks and values feedback from her employees and customers. She uses feedback to drive improvement and make strategic decisions.

**Steps:**

- ✓ Seek feedback from a trusted mentor, colleague, or friend.
- ✓ Listen attentively, take notes, and reflect on the feedback received.
- ✓ Use the feedback to improve and grow.

**Summary:** Develop a growth mindset, actively seek feedback from mentors or experts, listen without defensiveness, and use feedback as a tool for improvement.

**Practical Exercises to Encourage Active Engagement and Facilitate Self-reflection**

Attention to Feedback Exercise: The Feedback Reflection Instructions:

- ✓ Collect feedback from various sources, such as colleagues, friends, or mentors.
- ✓ Organize the feedback and identify recurring themes or areas for improvement.

- ✓ Develop a plan to address the feedback and make positive changes.
- ✓ Reflect on how implementing feedback contributes to your growth and development.

**Your Turn:**

*What Steps are you taking today in achieving this goal of becoming a Champion?*

# Day 27: Habit 27- Teamwork

*"Success is not just about making money. It's about making a difference."* - **Unknown**

Champions collaborate effectively with others, recognizing the power of synergy and collective effort. Example: Winning sports teams excel through coordinated teamwork and shared goals.

**Example:** Phil Jackson, the former professional basketball player, coach, and executive, who played 12 seasons in the NBA, winning NBA championships, fostered a strong team culture and emphasized teamwork during his coaching career. He led teams to multiple NBA championships by building trust and collaboration among players.

**Steps:**

- ✓ Engage in a collaborative project or task.
- ✓ Foster a positive team dynamic, contribute actively, and support others.
- ✓ Celebrate team achievements and recognize individual contributions.

**Summary:** Communicate openly and honestly, respect others' opinions, contribute actively, support teammates, and focus on team success rather than individual achievements.

**Practical Exercises to Encourage Active Engagement and Facilitate Self-reflection**

Teamwork Exercise: The Collaboration Project Instructions:

- ✓ Collaborate on a project or task with a group of colleagues or friends.

- ✓ Communicate openly and respectfully, seeking input from all team members.
- ✓ Identify and appreciate each member's contributions to the project.
- ✓ Evaluate the team's dynamics and communication to enhance future collaborations.

**Your Turn:**

*What Steps are you taking today in achieving this goal of becoming a Champion?*

# Day 28: Habit 28- Time for Rest and Recovery

*"Champions are made when no one is watching." -* **Unknown**

Champions understand the importance of rest and recovery to maintain peak performance and prevent burnout. Example: Elite athletes incorporate rest days and recovery techniques into their training schedules.

**Example:** LeBron James, a professional basketball player, recognizes the importance of rest and recovery in maintaining performance. He incorporates rest days, engages in recovery practices, and manages his workload to sustain his longevity in the sport.

**Steps:**

- ✓ Allocate a day or specific time for rest and relaxation.
- ✓ Engage in activities that help you recharge and rejuvenate.
- ✓ Prioritize self-care and ensure a healthy work-life balance.

**Summary:** Establish regular periods of rest, engage in activities that help you relax and recharge, prioritize sleep, and listen to your body's signals for rest.

**Practical Exercises to Encourage Active Engagement and Facilitate Self-reflection**

Time for Rest and Recovery Exercise: The Restorative Rituals Instructions:

- ✓ Create a list of restorative rituals that help you relax and recharge.
- ✓ Incorporate these rituals into your daily or weekly routine.
- ✓ Prioritize rest and recovery without feeling guilty or pressured to be constantly productive.
- ✓ Reflect on how these rituals improve your overall well-being and productivity.

**Your Turn:**

*What Steps are you taking today in achieving this goal of becoming a Champion?*

# Day 29: Habit 29- Decision-Making

*"Success is not the absence of failure; it's the persistence through failure."* - **Aisha Tyler**

Champions make informed and effective decisions, considering both short-term and long-term implications. Example: Successful entrepreneurs weigh risks and benefits before making crucial business decisions.

**Example:** Mary Barra, mentioned earlier, demonstrates strong decision-making skills as the CEO of General Motors. She makes informed decisions by considering relevant information and long-term implications for the company.

**Steps:**

- ✓ Confront a decision you have been avoiding or find challenging.
- ✓ Gather relevant information, weigh pros and cons, and make a well-informed decision.
- ✓ Reflect on the outcomes and learn from the decision-making process.

**Summary:** Gather relevant information, evaluate options, consider potential outcomes, consult with trusted advisors, and make decisions based on a balance of rationality and intuition.

**Practical Exercises to Encourage Active Engagement and Facilitate Self-reflection**

Decision-Making Exercise: The Decision Journal Instructions:

- ✓ Keep a journal of significant decisions you make.

- ✓ Document the options considered, the reasoning behind your choice, and the outcomes.
- ✓ Evaluate the effectiveness of your decision-making process and learn from past experiences.
- ✓ Use the journal to make more informed and thoughtful decisions in the future.

**Your Turn:**

*What Steps are you taking today in achieving this goal of becoming a Champion?*

# Day 30: Habit 30- Continuous Improvement

*"Champions are defined by how they handle defeat, not victory."* - **Unknown**

Champions constantly seek ways to improve their skills, knowledge, and performance. Example: Innovators refine and enhance their products based on user feedback and market demands.

**Example:** Jeff Weiner, an American businessman, who was the chief executive officer (CEO) of LinkedIn, embodies a commitment to continuous improvement. He actively seeks feedback, invests in personal growth, and fosters a learning culture within organizations.

**Steps:**

- ✓ Identify an aspect of your life or work that can be improved.
- ✓ Set goals for improvement and develop a plan to achieve them.
- ✓ Embrace a growth mindset and commit to ongoing learning and development.

**Summary:** Embrace a growth mindset, seek opportunities for learning and development, set specific improvement goals, and consistently challenge yourself to push beyond your comfort zone.

**Practical Exercises to Encourage Active Engagement and Facilitate Self-reflection**

Continuous Improvement Exercise: The Growth Mindset Plan Instructions:

- ✓ Develop a growth mindset plan that outlines your commitment to continuous improvement.
- ✓ Set specific goals for personal and professional development.
- ✓ Track your progress and celebrate milestones along your growth journey.
- ✓ Share your growth mindset plan with a close friend or mentor for support and accountability.

**Your Turn:**

*What Steps are you taking today in achieving this goal of becoming a Champion?*

# Day 31: Habit 31- Celebration and Reflection on Success

*"Success is not the key to happiness. Happiness is the key to success. If you love what you are doing, you will be successful."* - **Albert Schweitzer**

Champions acknowledge and celebrate their achievements, fostering motivation and gratitude. Example: Award-winning actors celebrate their successes and reflect on the journey that led them there.

**Example:** Mark Zuckerberg, the co-founder of Facebook, regularly reflects on the company's successes and failures. He celebrates milestones, learns from experiences, and adapts strategies for continued growth and innovation.

**Steps:**

- ✓ Reflect on your journey, accomplishments, and lessons learned.
- ✓ Celebrate your achievements and express gratitude for the support received.
- ✓ Set new goals and aspirations for the future.

**Summary:** Take time to appreciate your accomplishments, reflect on the lessons learned, express gratitude to those who supported you, and use past successes as fuel for future endeavors.

**Practical Exercises to Encourage Active Engagement and Facilitate Self-reflection**

Celebration and Reflection on Success Exercise: The Success Gratitude Letter Instructions:

- ✓ Write a gratitude letter to yourself, acknowledging your accomplishments and growth.
- ✓ Celebrate your successes, both big and small, and express gratitude for your efforts.
- ✓ Reflect on the challenges you overcame and the lessons you learned along the way.
- ✓ Keep the gratitude letter as a reminder of your journey to greatness.

**Your Turn:**
*What Steps are you taking today in achieving this goal of becoming a Champion?*

These real-life examples showcase how individuals from various fields have embodied the listed habits and leveraged them to achieve notable success.

Remember, this suggested schedule is a starting point, and you can adapt it to suit your needs and preferences. The key is to consistently practice and integrate these habits into your daily life, gradually building a strong foundation for personal growth and success.

## Building and Incorporating these Habits into Your Life

Here are some steps to help you develop and imbibe these habits:

- ✓ Assess your current habits: Identify areas where you can improve and select a few habits to focus on initially.
- ✓ Set specific goals: Determine what you want to achieve and break it down into actionable steps.
- ✓ Educate yourself: Read books, articles, and biographies of successful individuals who embody these habits.
- ✓ Start small: Begin by incorporating one habit at a time into your routine to avoid overwhelm and increase your chances of success.
- ✓ Create reminders: Use visual cues, such as sticky notes or smart-phone alarms, to remind yourself to practice the habits consistently.
- ✓ Track your progress: Keep a journal or use habit-tracking apps to monitor your development and hold yourself accountable.
- ✓ Seek support and accountability: Share your goals and progress with a trusted friend, mentor, or coach who can provide guidance and hold you accountable.
- ✓ Be patient and persistent: Building habits takes time and effort. Stay committed, even when faced with setbacks or challenges.
- ✓ Reflect and adjust: Regularly assess your progress, celebrate small wins, and make necessary adjustments to your approach.

Remember, building these habits is a lifelong journey. Stay committed to continuous improvement, adapt as needed, and embrace the process of personal growth.

# Conclusion: Becoming a Champion

Congratulations on completing **'31 Key Habits of Champions: Your 31-Day Journey to Greatness'!** We hope this book has been a valuable resource in your quest to cultivate the habits that lead to success and championship-level performance.

Throughout these pages, we have explored the habits that set champions apart—the mindset, behaviors, and practices that enable individuals to rise above the ordinary and achieve extraordinary results. From goal setting and discipline to adaptability and continuous improvement, each habit plays a crucial role in shaping the path to greatness.

It is important to recognize that becoming a champion is not a destination; it is an ongoing journey. Mastery of these habits takes time, effort, and commitment. As you incorporate these habits into your life, remember that progress is more important than perfection. Embrace the process of growth, learn from setbacks, and persist in your pursuit of excellence.

Champions understand that success is not solely measured by external accomplishments but by the person they become along the way. It is about the values they uphold, the impact they make, and the positive influence they have on others. As you develop these habits, let them guide you not only to personal achievements but also to a greater purpose—using your skills and talents to make a difference in the lives of others.

Remember, champions are not limited to specific fields or industries. They can be found in sports, business, arts, education, and countless other domains. What unites them is their unwavering commitment to excellence, their resilience in the face of adversity, and their relentless pursuit of growth.

As you conclude this journey, we encourage you to continue fostering these habits in your daily life. Make them an integral part of your routine, your decision-making process, and your interactions with others. Surround yourself with individuals who inspire and support your journey, and in turn, inspire and support them.

Finally, never forget the power you hold within. Each one of us has the potential to be a champion in our own unique way. Embrace your strengths, embrace your passions, and unleash your full potential. Believe in yourself, trust in your abilities, and never be afraid to dream big.

Thank you for joining us on this transformative exploration of the 31 key habits of champions. May these habits serve as your guiding principles on the path to success, fulfillment, and making a lasting impact.

Here's to your journey as a champion—may it be filled with growth, achievement, and the realization of your wildest aspirations.

***Go forth, embrace these habits, and become the Champion you were born to be!***

## About the Author 'GERARD ASSEY'

Gerard Assey is a Graduate in Economics, a PGD in Management (HRD) and holds a Doctorate in Leadership. Gerard holds several International Qualifications in Sales, Debt Collection, Training & Teaching, and is a 'Fellow' of the prestigious 'Institute of Sales & Marketing Management'-UK, a Certified NLP Practitioner, a 'Certified Trainer', an 'Accredited Management Teacher-Behavioral Sciences', a 'Certified Competency Facilitator', a 'Certified Management Consultant'- (the International credentials of a professional management consultant, awarded in accordance with global standards of the ICMCI); and a Certification from the University of Michigan in 'Successful Negotiation: Essential Strategies and Skills'

He is also a Member of the 'National Association of Sales Professionals' backed with several years experience in varied industries, both in India and Overseas. He also holds an 'Etiquette Consultant' Certification from the USA (by Sue Fox, Author of Best Seller: 'Business Etiquette for Dummies'. She has trained some of the top celebrities' world over). He was also a recipient of a scholarship for extensive training in Japan on 'Corporate Management for India'.

Gerard Assey is 'Founder & Chief Corporate Trainer' of the Group: **'Citius, Altius, Fortius Unlimited'**- an organization that **celebrated 20 years of Glorious Service** in 2021, focusing on 3 Core Competencies:

**People. Performance. Profit**; in functional areas of Sales & Marketing, HR & Organizational Development, covering Recruitment, Training & Consultancy!

Having managed organizations with large Sales Forces in India & Overseas, his specialization cover extensive areas of Sales Training (All levels - Presentation, Negotiation, Key/ Strategic Accounts Management & Managerial Skills for all sectors), Bid Proposal/ Capture Planning/ Management Trainings, Retail Sales, Customer Service & Customer Retention Programs, Training for Prevention & Collection of Debt, Self & Personal Development Programs (Time Management, Teamwork & Team Building, Business Etiquette & Personal Grooming, Leadership & Managerial Skills, People Management Skills, Train-the-Trainer etc), including preparation of Custom-designed Business Manuals for Internal (HR, Induction, and Sales etc) & External use (Instruction, User Manuals).

Gerard has successfully conducted over 5980 Trainings & Workshops (as of Sept '23) all across India, Middle East, Africa, Europe & S.E. Asia. Besides public programs conducted regularly, both in India & Overseas, he has some of the top names as clients whom he services from Single Owners to large Public & Government undertakings, covering all sectors, for their in-house needs.

His website: www.CollectionSkills.com is the only one in this part of the world to be featured in the 'Collections & Credit Risk Magazine-USA' under 'Who's Who in Training' and ranks TOP, along with other websites listed below on most search engines.

Gerard is author of 78 books already (Sept 2023),

**A few of the business related books being:**

1. Bite-sized Bits on Commonsense Management
2. Heart to Heart on Life's Principles'
3. How to become a Successful Manager
4. The Sales Professionals' Master Workbook of S.Y.S.T.E.M.S
5. The Professional Business Email Etiquette Handbook & Guide
6. The Professional Business Video-Conferencing Etiquette Handbook & Guide
7. Professional Presentation Skills
8. Exceptional Customer Service
9. Professional Tele-Marketing Skills
10. Professional Debt Collection Skills
11. The G.R.E.A.T. Sales & Service Workbook
12. Sales Training Advantage for Results (*The Ultimate Sales Training Manual to enable you stand out as a S.T.A.R.*)
13. CEO Daily Planner & Organizer
14. The Sales Professionals' Master Daily Planner
15. The Professional Debt Collector's Master Daily Planner
16. My Daily Planner & Organizer
17. MY EMERGENCY INFORMATION RECORD (Family Emergency & Peace of Mind Planner)
18. The Ultimate Therapist & Counselors Planner and Organizer
19. Building an Ethical Workplace
20. Managing Relationships at Work
21. Managing Business Meetings Effectively
22. Effective Delegation Skills
23. Goal Setting for Success
24. B2B Selling by Email
25. Professional Business Etiquette & Grooming
26. Dining Etiquette & Table Manners
27. Effective Networking Skills

28. Grooming, Etiquette & Manners for Teens, Young Adults & Future Leaders
29. Inter-Personal Skills
30. Get Ready, Get Hired!
31. Selling in a Recession
32. Effective Receivables Management in an Economic Downturn!
33. Real Estate & Property Sales Training
34. Credit Sales & Accounts Receivable Management
35. Selling Skills for Real Estate & Property Advisors
36. Take G.R.E.A.T. C.A.R.E!
37. Spa, Salon & Health Club Selling Skills
38. Selling Travel, Holiday & MICE Services
39. Selling Skills for Spa's, Salons & Health Clubs
40. Retailing in Salons & Spas
41. Selling Holiday, Vacation, Tours & Packages
42. The Power of Sales Referrals
43. Selling Luxury
44. Technical Selling Skills Financial Advisors Sales Training
45. Dealing with Burnout at Work
46. Monopolize Your Markets
47. Selling to Affluent Customers
48. Financial Selling Skills
49. *The Effective Manager's Guide: Key Skills to Thrive*
50. From Aspiring to Inspiring: A Guide for New Managers on the Rise
51. The Power of Focus
52. Selling with Integrity: Sell Like Jesus The Perfect Role Model!
53. 31 Habits of Champions: Your 31-Day Journey to Greatness

Besides regularly contributing to business & trade journals, including international ones such as the 'Creative Training Techniques' and the 'Sales News' of the U.S.A, He is also a member of several prestigious bodies & trade associations, having participated in many Conferences & Workshops in India & Overseas.

Prior to his last assignment of leading & managing a large MNC as head, Gerard had a 3-year stint in the Middle East as a Consultant with a leading British Consultancy Firm.

As the past 'Official Country Representative' for the International Business Award- 'THE STEVIES'-(the business world's own Oscar) for about 4 years- he ensured a few Indian companies that qualify for the same every year!

Gerard can be contacted at:

Email: training@Sales-Training.in,training@CollectionSkills.com
Websites:

www.Sales-Training.in
www.EtiquetteWorks.in
www.CollectionSkills.com
www.RetailSalesTraining.in
www.SalesTrainingIndia.com
www.ManualPreparation.com
www.TrainingWithPuppets.com
www.FirstContactAcademy.com
www.SalesAndMarketingRecruiter.com

## Our TRAININGS & BOOKS that can help your team

- ✓ **Sales Effectiveness**: Selling Skills for any Sector: Service/ Logistics/ FMCG Realty/ Insurance & Finance/ Media/ SPA's, Health Clubs & Salons/ Key Account Management, Effective Negotiation Skills/ Bid & Proposal Management Skills/ Retail Sales Training: Any Sector (Auto, Jewelry, Clothing, Luxury etc)
- ✓ **Customer Service Skills**-Complaints Handling & Customer Retention
- ✓ **Debt Prevention & Collection Skills**
- ✓ **Etiquette & Grooming**
- ✓ **Leadership & Managerial Skills**
- ✓ **Self & Personal Development Skills**: Presentation Skills/ Effective Communication Skills/Business Proposal Writing Skills/ Problem Solving & Decision Making Skills/ Empowering Secretaries-The perfect PA! (For Secretaries & PA's)/ Effective Time Management/ Teamwork & Teambuilding/ P.R.I.D.E- **P**ersonal **R**esponsibility **I**n **D**elivering **E**xcellence

A Few of Our Business Books
By the Top Corporate Trainer & Author of 77 Books! (Sep '23)
And...DAILY PLANNERS for Every Corporate Need!
All Books available Online on all leading Stores in E-book & Paperback Formats
Experts in Training for over 22 years:
Sales, Debt Prevention & Collection, Etiquette & Grooming ,
Leadership & Managerial Skills, Self & Personal Development Programs
By the Top Corporate Trainer (Over 5980 workshops)
& Author of 77 Published Books (Sep'23)

www.ingramcontent.com/pod-product-compliance
Lightning Source LLC
LaVergne TN
LVHW010455160826
845677LV00012B/2493

* 9 7 8 9 3 9 2 4 9 2 7 1 6 *